Julia Caesar

Written by Ciaran Murtagh

Illustrated by Olga Demidova

Introduction

Julius Caesar lived from 100 to 44 BCE.
For a time, he was the most powerful man
in the world. He had many enemies.
One of those enemies was called Brutus.
Julia was Julius's daughter.

These characters have been used in this
story. They were real – but the story isn't!

OXFORD
UNIVERSITY PRESS

OXFORD
UNIVERSITY PRESS

Great Clarendon Street, Oxford, OX2 6DP, United Kingdom

Oxford University Press is a department of the University
of Oxford. It furthers the University's objective of excellence
in research, scholarship, and education by publishing
worldwide. Oxford is a registered trade mark of Oxford
University Press in the UK and in certain other countries

Text © Ciaran Murtagh 2015
Illustrations © Olga Demidova 2015

The moral rights of the author have been asserted

First published 2015

British Library Cataloguing in Publication Data
Data available

ISBN: 978-0-19-835679-0

10 9 8 7 6 5 4 3

Paper used in the production of this book is a natural, recyclable product
made from wood grown in sustainable forests. The manufacturing process
conforms to the environmental regulations of the country of origin.

Printed in China by Leo Paper Products Ltd

Acknowledgements

Series Advisor: Nikki Gamble

CHAPTER I

Julia wriggled as the dressmaker worked.

"Stay still!" said Julia's mum. "You always fidget when you're having a new gown fitted!"

"That's because I don't like gowns," said Julia. "Why do I need a new one?"

"Because we're going to the feast tonight,"
said Julia's mum. "The daughter of Julius Caesar
has to look her best."

Julia grumbled as she looked in the mirror.
The gown was pink and covered in flowers.
She hated it. Sometimes being the daughter
of the most powerful man in the world was
a difficult job!

"I look so … *girly*," said Julia. "It hasn't even got a pocket for my lucky marble."

Mum was about to say something when Julia's dad, Julius, marched in.

"You look lovely," he said as he picked up Julia. "Perfect for Brutus's feast! He's promised me a big surprise tonight."

Julia screwed up her face. If there was one thing she hated more than gowns and feasts, it was Brutus.

"Don't pull that face," laughed Dad, setting Julia down on the floor. "He's not that bad."

"He's worse," muttered Julia, as she struggled out of her gown and back into her comfy tunic. "Can I go and play now?" she asked.

Mum nodded.

"But stay away from Marcus," she said. "The daughter of Julius Caesar shouldn't play with servants!"

7

Julia found Marcus outside, scrubbing the steps of the villa. Mum didn't like her to play with Marcus because he was a servant. But Julia didn't care – Marcus was her age and they were friends.

"Have you got time for a game, Marcus?" she asked.

"Not yet," said Marcus. "Your mum wants me to clean these steps."

"I'll help." Julia took another brush and bent down to scrub, too.

When the steps were sparkling, Julia smiled.

"Now can we play?" she asked. She ran towards the gate. "Catch me if you can!"

Marcus chased Julia across the courtyard, through the market and down an alleyway.

"You're too fast!" laughed Marcus.

Julia ran up some steps onto the roof of a house. Soon they were leaping from

rooftop

to

rooftop.

"Slow down!" cried Marcus.
"I'll never catch you!"

"That's the idea!" laughed Julia, as she leaped over a chimney.

Marcus crept around the other side of the
chimney and tagged Julia's shoulder.

"Got you!" he said.

They were about to start again, when Julia
heard someone talking below them.

"Let's see who it is," she whispered, and they
crawled towards the edge of the roof.

CHAPTER II

Down below, Brutus and his two favourite servants, Felix and Claudius, were standing in a shadowy corner of the square.

"Here's the letter," whispered Brutus, looking over his shoulder to check nobody was listening.

On the roof, Julia and Marcus listened as Felix read the letter out loud.

"I, Julius Caesar, resign as the leader of Rome ..."

Claudius put up his hand. "What does 'resign' mean?"

"It means he's giving up his job," explained Felix.

"Which would make me the leader of Rome," said Brutus. "I'm second in command, after all."

"But Julius would never give up his job," said Claudius, scratching his head.

"Not on purpose," laughed Brutus. "I tricked him. He thought he was signing something else. I'm going to show this letter to everybody at the feast tonight."

Up above, Julia couldn't believe her ears. Her heart began to pound.

"We have to stop them!" she whispered.

But Brutus wasn't finished. "One more thing," he said. "I have had a cake made to celebrate my new job. Bring it to the feast."

"We have to get that letter," said Marcus,
running towards the stairs.

He was in such a hurry, he slipped
and slid
towards the
edge of the roof.

Julia grabbed his arm but it was too late.

Marcus fell – and pulled his best friend with him. Julia closed her eyes as they

tumbled

towards

the ground.

Julia cried out in fear as they fell ...
just before she and Marcus landed in
a fountain, with a

splash!

Julia opened her eyes. She
and Marcus were both wet but
they weren't hurt. Brutus turned
to look in their direction.

"What was that?" Brutus asked.

Julia pulled Marcus back under the water.

"Probably a cat or something," said Claudius.

Brutus gave the fountain one last look
and marched off across the square. Felix and
Claudius followed.

Julia was still hiding. She heard Brutus and the servants walking away. When she was sure they were gone, she burst out of the water.

"We need to tell someone," panted Julia, as she clambered out of the fountain. She ran towards the palace and Marcus chased after her.

CHAPTER III

"Look at the state of you!" said Mum when Julia burst into the room.

Julia looked. Her tunic was wet through and she was leaving a trail of puddles on the floor. Marcus arrived by her side.

"I might have known you'd have something to do with this!" Mum snapped at Marcus.

He scurried out.

"Mum, I need to tell you something," said Julia.

But Mum was too angry to listen.

"I told you not to play with him!" she said.
"Thank goodness your new gown is finished.
Go and get changed this instant!"

"But we can't go to the feast," spluttered Julia. "Brutus is ..."

"Enough," said Mum. "You're going to the feast and you're going to get changed.

NOW!"

Julia opened her mouth to speak again but Mum had turned to leave.

As the dressmaker helped Julia into her gown, she showed Julia a secret pocket she had added. "For your lucky marble," she whispered.

Julia thanked the dressmaker and put the marble in the pocket. It made the bad dress a little bit better.

She was only just ready when her parents called her. It was time to go.

Their chariot sped out of the palace towards Brutus's villa. Marcus held the reins. As they raced across the square, Julia tried to persuade her parents to turn around.

"We have to go back!" she begged. *"Please!"*

Julius chuckled as he waved to the
cheering crowd.

"You really don't like feasts, do you Julia?"
he said.

"It's not the feast," said Julia. "It's ..."

But before she had a chance to explain,
trumpet music filled the air. They had arrived.
  The dining room was covered in flowers.
It looked like the whole of Rome had come
to the feast.

Marcus had to go and help in the
kitchen, and Brutus sat down next to Julia.

Julia gave him a nasty stare and moved her
chair away a little. She had to stop his wicked
plan – but how?

CHAPTER IV

All through the meal, Julia tried to warn Mum and Dad about Brutus's plan. But whenever she started, they were talking to someone important.

Once the final course was finished, Brutus got to his feet and clapped his hands. The room fell silent.

Julia's heart began to race.

Was this it?

"Soon it will be time for my surprise," said Brutus. "But first – music!"

In the corner a band began to play. The floor was filled with dancers. Julia breathed a sigh of relief – she still had time.

Mum got to her feet.
"Shall we dance, Julius?"

Julius was about to stand when Brutus stopped him.

"No," said Brutus. "He has to stay here for his surprise."

"Oh yes," smiled Julius. "I don't want to miss my surprise. Why don't you dance with Julia, darling?" he said to Mum.

Julia didn't want to dance! She needed to be near Brutus. Maybe she would get a chance to tear up the letter when he pulled it from his pocket.

But before she could do anything, Mum grabbed her arm and pulled her onto the dance floor.

As she spun around the dance floor, Julia saw Brutus rummaging in his pocket. It was almost time!

She had to do something – but what?

CHAPTER V

Brutus took the folded letter from his pocket. He was going to read it out loud to everybody. Julia had to tear it up!

Julia couldn't stand it any more. She wriggled out of her mother's hands and dashed through the dancers towards Brutus. But no matter how hard she tried, she always seemed to find herself spun by the dancers, back to where she had started.

Julia crouched and tried to crawl through the dancers' legs. But it was no use.

Brutus clapped his hands and the music stopped. He unfolded the letter and cleared his throat. Felix and Claudius were waiting nearby, ready with the cake.

"Ladies and gentlemen," said Brutus, holding up the letter. "I have something to show you."

Julia closed her eyes. Brutus was about to become the leader of Rome and there was nothing she could do about it.

It was then she felt something digging into her leg. Her lucky marble! She needed a distraction and she knew exactly what to do.

Julia took the marble from her pocket and aimed carefully. Just as the dancers' legs made a perfect tunnel, she rolled it across the floor.

It was a brilliant shot. The marble skidded under Claudius's foot and suddenly he was falling.

"Whoa!" he cried, grabbing Felix
for support.

Felix began to fall, too.

"Watch it!" he shouted as the cake
flew into the air and ...

... landed on Brutus.

SPLAT!

In the confusion, the letter flew from Brutus's hand and fluttered across the dance floor. While everyone laughed at Brutus, Julia ran and grabbed it, stuffing it into her hidden marble pocket.

"You **fools!**" shouted Brutus, shaking crumbs from his hair. "Can't you get *anything* right?"

It was then he realized he'd dropped something.

"Where's the letter?" he gasped. Julia patted her secret pocket and smiled. She'd done it.

CHAPTER VI

The feast ended very suddenly after that.
Brutus, still covered in cake, chased his
two servants around the room, which made
everybody laugh even harder.

In the chariot on the way home,
Julius turned to his daughter.
"Do you still dislike feasts,
Julia?" he asked.

Julia giggled and shook her head.

"That one was the best ever," she laughed.
"And if Brutus got splatted with cake every
time, I'd go every day!"

"And you'd wear that gown?" asked Mum.
"I wouldn't wear anything else," said
Julia, thinking of her secret pocket with the
letter hidden inside.

When she got home, Julia threw Brutus's letter into the fire. As she watched it burn, she smiled. Being the daughter of the most powerful man in Rome wasn't so bad after all.